New Poems

New Poems

THOMAS TRZYNA

RESOURCE *Publications* · Eugene, Oregon

NEW POEMS

Copyright © 2020 Thomas Trzyna. All rights reserved. Except for brief quotations in critical publications or reviews, no part of this book may be reproduced in any manner without prior written permission from the publisher. Write: Permissions, Wipf and Stock Publishers, 199 W. 8th Ave., Suite 3, Eugene, OR 97401.

Resource Publications
An Imprint of Wipf and Stock Publishers
199 W. 8th Ave., Suite 3
Eugene, OR 97401

www.wipfandstock.com

PAPERBACK ISBN: 978-1-7252-7991-9
HARDCOVER ISBN: 978-1-7252-7990-2
EBOOK ISBN: 978-1-7252-7992-6

Manufactured in the U.S.A.   07/29/20

These poems are for the late Rose Reynoldson. Her careful and kind critiques raised many poets from nothing. She grew up outside Florence Acres in the Depression. That's uphill from Woods Creek in the forest beyond Monroe, Washington, where the state prison broods over the town. Her family made its way by brewing hooch and holding weekend dances. Somehow, she finished graduate school and became a professor. Her book, *I know There's Something More*, tells about rough love and strong religion.

I dedicate this book also to Martha, my love of 50 years, who was taken by the Covid virus. Her poems are to come.

These are new poems because there are a couple of dozen old ones in print here and there. All I claim is that these are worth reading twice because I attend to meaning, meter and music.

My name is an obstacle. It means 'reed' in Polish, and it's pronounced something like Chinna. It's onomatopoetic. Think of a sea of dry reed stalks clicking against each other in a wind, or the sea of reeds Moses may have parted with his refugees. There's a river like that between Poland and Czechia.

The poems are divided into two groups: Lands and People, and Abstractions and Ideas.

Contents

Proem: Threnody in Time
   of Plague | 1

Lands and People | 3
Afterwards | 5
Santa Cruz | 7
Ten Mile Creek,
   Sierra Nevada | 9
Sorrento Valley | 10
Scrub Oaks | 11
Hotel Winnedumah | 12
Ishi | 14
Swans Gone | 15
Black's Beach | 16
Homestead | 17
Oakland | 18
Roommates | 19
Adobe Flores | 21
For Yvor Winters | 23
Professor Iguana | 24
Uncle Max's Mandolin | 25
Requiem for a Boxer | 26
In Memory of Mama's | 27
Muscat | 28
Hanoi | 29
One Grandfather | 30
Parrots | 31
On Lamplight | 32

Proletarian Poet | 33
Tanka | 35
Flying Fortress | 36
Quercus | 37
The Home of Truth | 38

Ideas and Abstractions | 41
Aeschylus Knew Better | 43
Poetry Weather | 44
Henge | 45
Poetry Time | 46
Communion | 47
Objecting | 48
QED (Quantum
   Electrodynamics) | 49
Near Telegraph | 50
On the Anniversary
   of People's Park | 51
Oud | 52
Baglama | 53
Swallow | 54
Euler's Identity | 55
I am Life and Death | 56
Dame Julian | 57
Variation on Verses
   from Jonah and Job | 58
That Tree | 59
Teaching | 60
It is What it Is | 61
Bad Times | 62
Glass Butte, Oregon | 63

The Artichoke | 64
General Education | 65
September 1, 2019 | 66
Canzone | 67
Holy | 69
Design | 71

Baby Boomer | 72
Covid 19, or The Revenge
　of the Pangolin | 73
Envoy: Now Rose | 74

Old Poems | 75

Proem: Threnody in Time of Plague

British Museum, London, March 10, 2020

> "Timor mortis conturbat me."
> —*Lament for the Makaris,*
>   *William Dunbar, 16th century*

The news was never false, though lately
Speculation filled the pages. Now, fatally,
There's no news at all, just silence
That throws us back on self-reliance.
      Pax mortis consolat me.

The answer is, we do not know.
Antarctic ice speeds its flow.
The virus harvests a large percent
Of folks who quailed and quickly went.
      Pax mortis consolat me.

The quarantined complain of loneliness
Though Netflix fills the air no less.
Somehow virtual companions pale
When living at home resembles jail.
      Pax mortis consolat me.

Membership, begin with that.
So goes Pascal's fine dictat.
The bell that tolls, tolls for you.
You must assume that burden too.
      Pax mortis consolat me.

Alone with the vases in the British Museum
Pondering Keats' famous dictum,
Blaise's wisdom seems more germane.
We need others to keep us sane.
   Amor hominum consolat me.

And something more called active love.
"Enough sentimentality! Quit it, Gov!"
Really? It's self-evident.
We need our friends to be content.
   Amor hominum consolat me.

The whole's more than the sum of parts,
Stats and grim mortality charts,
Statues missing lips and noses,
Politicos and their odious poses.
   Amor hominum consolat me.

In fact, I'd rather like to think
Something larger forms a link.
Call it what you won't—or will.
Alone or fellowed, busy or still:
   Amor dei consolat nos.
   Love sustains us.

Lands and People

Afterwards

Whether they be high or low, the future
Seas will wash shores somewhere, shelves of shale
Wear and crack, sandstone dissolve to dunes,
Crustaceans scuttle, the sibilance of surf
Break silence, the shift of shingle in the shallows
Excite at night a neon phosphorescence,
Morning light cast shadows of sculpted crests
Of sand that tides will set in sweeping crescents.
Flecks of foam will sere to grains of salt,
Crabs leave scuffs and scratches where they crawl,
Offshore flows waft in forests of kelp.
Some scrubs will survive, short and sharp,
With barbs and bitter leaves adapted to
Immersion when storm-reared breakers rush
And crash, driving dense deadwood deep
Up beaches. Urchins and sea stars, blue and orange,
May tint the broad serene. The brine will still
Be sticky, the water chill to foraging species
Come down from fractured bluffs and limestone caves.

There will be dry oases, moist enough
Deep down to sustain some thirsty palms.
Their fronds will shade narrow canyons along
Late littorals now home to sage and dust.
In winter, rainfall on steep aretes will
Run to recurring springs and marshy hollows
Where with care and effort, a palmful of turbid
Water might fill a freshly dug pit.
Areca kernels reduced to paste in granite
Mortars, the skin and pulp consumed at once:
These will be the favored foods, with roasted
Locusts and wild onions. Few groves of palms

Will survive the age of searing heat and drought,
The populations they support small
And imperiled, an equilibrium
Familiar to the Kumayaay and Piaute.

Santa Cruz

She bought the wind-blasted cottage with the proceeds
From her portraits, the ones she chose to sell.
She hoarded special canvases that harshly
Unmasked supercilious scholars who sat
Content for pictures in her studio,
Unaware of the doubles and triples she later
Daubed to reveal the ugly truths she sensed
Behind their faces. Those she stashed away
In a narrow closet built for hiding liquor
During Prohibition, back of a sliding
Panel at their home in Palo Alto.
Formidable was an accurate assessment
Of her character. The beach house, built
On a slope of sand that shifted in the frequent
Quakes, had floors that slanted and a roof that spread,
Admitting rain and even heavy dew.
Beneath the rafters, she and our uncle positioned
Lines of cups and pans and pots to catch
The drips and flows that dried each searing summer.
Chairs and tables tilted, rocked and tipped,
Dishes spilled their contents, playing cards
Slid softly to the gouged pine floors,
A serendipity that led to flagrant,
Hilarious cheating in games of Boston Rummy,
Bridge, and fast-paced 'Spite and Malice.'
The rough-hewn quarter-sawn redwood planks
That stood as walls were finished inside with panels:
Square Deal Board dating from Teddy
Roosevelt's time. The house was listed on the Historic
Register: it could not be trued or altered,
Though like a weathered ship it needed hauling out.
At dusk we walked the railway trestle across

The river to the Boardwalk, watching our feet,
Stepping on uneven tar-black ties. Below,
The shallow current ebbed and rose with the tides.
Under the bright lights of the carnival games,
Eleanor, our maiden aunt, her fingers
Tacky with toffee, played whack-a-mole with childlike
Glee, laughing aloud at every hammer
Stroke, just as she pounded out Chopin on quivering
Keys, executing the Nocturnes forte,
The way she played the stately March Militaire.
Our uncle told how he fell in frigid tidepools,
Foraging for specimens among
Sharp and slippery rocks, of rogue waves
Roaring in from Monterey Bay,
Of Steinbeck and Doc Ricketts, the Hopkins Marine
Station and his loves: sea slugs, protozoans,
And sea cucumbers. Slimy samples stocked
Aquaria back at his Stanford lab,
Where some dawns he serenaded them,
Playing Bach's six cello suites by heart.
Behind the house a mound of glistening shells
Evoked the years when abalone flourished,
The Mother of Pearl shining in the sunlight.
Cuisine was basic, as in her childhood at her parents'
Farm outside Vidin, on the Danube, where meals
Roasted on a fire in the yard, their only kitchen,
And where watermelons, potatoes and cabbages
Filled the cavernous, cold, earthen cellar.
How peaceful, how dynamic the retreat
They crafted in their later years, after
Fleeing from Sofia on the last
Orient Express headed westward
Out of Istanbul in September '39.

Ten Mile Creek, Sierra Nevada

Some youthful judgments are correct.
Little in life excelled those idle hours
Face down on the polished, searing granite,
Watching the steam rise as the icy water
From that pool at Mylander Falls dried
Off our burning bodies: the laugh, the plunge.

Sorrento Valley

A sand bar bounds the stale marsh
Trapped between the mesas. Harsh
Nitrous bubbles burst and rise,
A narrow channel admits the tides
Rising from La Jolla Trench.
Whipping winter rainstorms drench
Dead yellow reeds whose broken shafts
Pierce sun-baked algae mats.
East, the tracks of the Santa Fe
Cut off the once broad bay.
Above these shallows where willets wade,
The Torrey pines cast their shade.
Inland, the two-lane asphalt track,
Thick with sand, winds crookedly back
Past idled farms and chicken shacks,
Rusty RVs and drying tack.
Motionless horses watch a dog slink low,
Its feathered muzzle white as snow.
At a bend a sun-bleached Coke machine
Brings back a time that must have been,
When the highway snaked past produce sheds
And GIs from boot camp hoed Victory beds.
Now, beyond a final turn, a dusty grove,
A pet cemetery eyed by crows,
And monuments set in narrow rows.

Scrub Oaks

Quercus Wislizeni, Sierra Nevada Foothills

Sometimes, when you brush their branches, they break,
Weakened by parasitic mistletoe,
Sparse rain, hard soil, and piercing sun.
Seen from these foothills, the Central Valley burns,
A haze of crop dust, smoke, and fog.
Biplanes buzz the fields, spewing spray.
Here, yellow stubble covers the soil.
The oaks lean at angles, their black limbs
As if flailing in all directions, seeking moisture.
Timid deer bed beneath their cover.
You cannot climb these trees. They shatter and crack.
This is a barrenness, unfit for citrus,
Produce, grapes, timber, grass, or hay.
Ten acres of this fodder serve to feed
A single thirsty cow. Predators
Descend from higher elevations, alert
And halting: bobcats, lions and wild boar,
Their tracks dried hard in winter mud.
Soon they favor more fecund hunting grounds.
The scrubs remain: wildflowers bloom and fade.
In shimmering heat, the oaks cast pale shade.

Hotel Winnedumah

Independence, California

At the old hotel, before the roof collapsed,
Its beams overtaxed by mounds of snow and ice,
Two faded sofas flanked the sooty hearth,
A cavernous arch crafted of granite boulders
Big as barrels. A Lilliputian flame
Flickered below the bent black grate;
The cushions sagged in scallops like the slick saddles
Roy Rogers and his partners rode when they came
To film two-reelers in grainy black and white:
The guys in white hats beat the black hats hollow.
Winnedumah means 'stand where you are,'
And so the Paiutes did 'til they were hunted,
And so the settlers tried until their water
Was shunted to dry L.A. And so the Nisei,
Who spent the war imprisoned at Manzanar.
Across the road, the courthouse stands for law,
Though the farmers lost their water rights,
The natives their lives, and the Japanese their livings.
Beyond the courthouse rise the barren Whites,
Mountains where remnants of the tribes escaped
The genocide before the Ghost Dance times,
Women huddled in icy, fireless caves,
Afraid to show a trace of rising smoke,
Men dead or fled to other climes
Or moved by force to the sere Tehachapis.
Wovoka, a local, prophesied revenge;
A few still dance his skeleton ritual.
Visitors drop pennies in the wind-
Scoured graveyard at the concentration camp,
Small signs of sorrow and sad respect.

The desk clerk cradled his fifth of clear tequila
In the shadow of the slumping stuccoed roof
That hung above the porch like final judgment,
A second bottle inside, beside the pad
That served as register and comment book.
Above the peaks, clouds cluster from bleak
To black, flashes of sunbeams break gold and red,
A wind blasts up the darkening desert valley
Through Mary Austin's land of little rain.
Where is it that the Winnedumah stands?

Ishi

When Ishi, the last survivor of the Yahi,
Sat down before an Edison wax recorder,
He spent twenty-four hours reciting the tales
Of Wood Duck, his tribe's totemic animal.
Not Neptune or Ares, Mars or Apollo, Wolf
Or Eagle, but gentle green-helmeted wood duck,
A monogamous bird that nests in riverain caves,
Whose adventures, no doubt, explained the Yahi
Custom of different dialects for men
And women, and their expectations for the after world,
Where life continues quietly underground,
A revelation for those whose myths are bloody
And whose hells are marred by endless tortures.
He learned his lore from his mother's lips
Those years in hiding, when they lived alone,
The rest left dead to rot above the soil,
Slaughtered by farmers whose belts hung heavy with scalps.
What other tales would Ishi have recorded?

Swans Gone

Where the piers of Yesler's sawmill stood,
Reduced to rotten stumps of wood,
Swans slept and raised their downy broods.
Vigilant and prone to moods
They hissed or lunged or tucked their necks.
The giant pens warmed their nests.
Blue herons watched—still, motionless,
While turtles on sunken logs processed
And pairs of faithful ducks and drakes
Bobbed in waves and rolling wakes.
Reeds encircled the round lagoon
Placid from morn to noon. Too soon:
What wild winter weather wasted
That world where paddlers had often tasted
The swamp alive with fox, raccoon?
Swans gone, all gone, the rising moon
Now lights a mirror, a barren shallow
Erased, expunged, bereft, unhallowed.

Black's Beach

Kumayaay in Ipai means
Those who face the water from
The cliffs: who sheltered from storms
In canyons home to rattlesnakes;
Who ate the urchins, seals and sharks
That grew or beached or swam too close;
Who clad their limbs in woven grasses
And drew their water in baskets tightly
Tied with needles from Torrey pines.
No more. The Spanish seized the land;
Salk's Institute spans the mesa.

We also watch wide oceans from the heights,
Observe the sea engulf low isles;
Gaze at stars now cold and dead;
See brilliant novae flash and spread;
Temperate forests burn to red,
The Amazon add its acrid smoke
To fires that the tundras stoke.
For those who face the water, the ledge
Is crumbling. We walk the edge.

Homestead

North of the headwaters of Yesler creek
The hillside bursts: twenty-one springs
Ooze into the quiet streets.
Our neighbor capped his well, a shallow shaft
Lined with brick and mortar, wide and full,
A mirror darkened by sediment and leaves.
Digging a fresh foundation, we snagged the iron
Rim of a discarded wagon wheel
And found—less likely—a silver spoon
From a posh tearoom of a Bournemouth hotel.
No Native plunder. A relic, perhaps,
Of a local airman who fought from England
And flew from the Naval Air Station, east,
Over the hill, where once the Pan Am Clippers
Ascended en route to Asia, their wide wakes
Roiling Lake Washington's waters. Orchards and a park
Displaced an Italian's produce farm. Then:
Three generations of houses: tiny post-war
Bungalows, shambling split-levels,
And now, new-century boxes with flat tops.
Chimneys give way to solar panels.
Yet still the creek, daylighting down the block,
Still the marsh and horse tails, reeds,
Wild berries, pines, and hidden salal.

Oakland

Our universes barely touched. Buck Paden's
Unpainted house had a sub-floor, no more.
Two steel chairs stood at a chipped
Formica table. Two pots and a fry pan,
A floppy mattress and a single knitted throw,
An extra suit of clothes. That was all.
Next to his lunch box at the hospital's
Gardening shed, he pinned that famous picture
Of Emmett Till, disfigured in his open
Casket. Buck grew giant onions and beans
On a toxic landfill between two steel plants
In Emeryville and wept at radio sermons.
He farmed as if he had not fled his land
In Alabama and mumbled as he worked.
We ate our sandwiches, silent in the face
Of the stories he chose to share of his escape.
On Telegraph, that student cavalcade,
Harald went bare black chested in mid-
December, so stoned he felt no cold.
He stashed the drugs he sold in the forks of trees,
While Rafa, six foot ten, including his Afro,
Stuffed the seats of his Jag sedan with parking
Tickets, the least of his long list of perils.
One could pretend to understand. Yet who
Would dare to ask those two grim guards
In heavy overcoats who stood beside
The entrance to that brick apartment block
In no man's land, where even the police
Seemed never to patrol, their angry faces
Fixed in dark disdain? Compared to them
The very Panthers looked Commedia dell'arte.

Roommates

2404 Dana, Berkeley

How apposite that you two wed,
Though only briefly. His forebears arrived
With cruel Pizarro, who fed the Inca
Molten gold, while yours settled
Greenwich Village and cleared a farm.
His father fought the Shining Path
And ruled the riotous state of Lima.
Yours regaled the Harvard Club
And married when it fit his mood.
Sweet refuge, Academe.
Your unruly sibs all died
By drugs or drew sentences in court,
While you achieved that pauper's safety,
Tenured posts in Europe and a coast.

Roy came from another class,
His dad a factory worker, a one
Bath house on the ragged edge
Of vast L.A. His uncle
Ollie led the communist youth
Through the Great Depression, met
Lenin in Moscow, and helped Svetlana
Settle in the U.S.A.—
Before he veered and joined John Birch.
A lifelong Quaker, Roy ripped
Off his robe to harangue his peers
At graduation. Dispirited
By the pace of racial progress,

He blew glass bongs, did time,
Got stoned each morning to teach
Mathematics in a public high,
And died of coke and crystal meth.

Rebecca, Gershon Legman's 'Aztec
Princess,' bragged one morning, smiling,
How her lover—Seven times!—
He'd just come back from
A tour of duty. 'Make love, not war:'
Legman coined that pregnant phrase.
She publicized the Brown Berets,
Read *Ramparts* like religion,
Marched in Oakland on the Day
To End the Draft, a riot where
The cops sprayed tear gas
Into her open eyes. Designer,
Promoter, inciter, she taught
Across the nation, East and South.
Now she lives with cats and lobbies
For Latina justice still.

Jimmy, stuttering, shows his sheaf
Of laminated children's pictures.
Of all his zigs and zags, his oddest
Was that hike alone in Burma's
Ethnic war zones, carrying
A backpack of colored pens
And paper for kids in hidden
Rebel camps. 'Draw what you want.'
Corpses, fire, exploding huts,
Bombs falling, severed limbs.

Adobe Flores

South Pasadena, California

From the Adobe Flores, El General could view
Dry hills rolling to a flatland. Out
Of sight lay the sea. The scent of grasses
Tickled his nose, while a horse neighed, and cattle
Grazed at leisure far enough away
Their odors never spoiled his days. Fremont
And Stockton, those American upstarts, had won
Their little war. Mexico must retreat.
He leaned against his door. Once Governor
Of California, he had packed
To leave. How large and small a matter, that battle
At Rio San Gabriel. Nine hundred men,
Four dead. January, 1847.
A mild winter. Oaks cast discs of shade.
The victors had threatened to shoot him. He must evade
Patrols, close the villa, and abandon his gardens.

A century passed. General Flores could still have viewed
The distant hills and taken his horses out
To ride the gentler slopes and graze the grasses,
Though houses had replaced the herds of cattle
And the famous ostrich farm had passed away.
A school now bore his name, and General Fremont
Had become an avenue. Who won?
Now speculators beat a quick retreat:
Their scams had come to light. The government,
With federal aid, worked slowly to unpack
The tangle of vertical lots, and win the battle

Of deeds and claims and trusts, so that men
Could build in those hills. Six or seven
Squatters lived along a creek in the shade
Of white-barked willows. In time they would evade
Eviction, remove their rabbits, and abandon their gardens.

For Yvor Winters

An oceanic sibilance.
Ebb and flood, faint florescence.
Hush. Last low rays light
The facets of rose sand crystals,
Each surface set apart: sheer cliffs
Blinding, brilliant. The sun sinks.
Sea birds scavenge the foamy shore.
A chill descends. The soft susurrus
Amplifies the night, the presence.

Professor Iguana

Professor Iguana flicks a page, reads
A line of Borges, thinks of sweet Lolita.
Humbert would envy him that pert conchita—
If only she would toss her rosary beads!
Iguana was abstemious by nature:
Devotions, alcohol, tobacco—none
Passed his lips. At four a brisk tisane
Awakes his spirit, keeps his focus pure.
How slowly, how delectably the years
Had passed: the quarry ever fresh and young,
Idolatrous as the tropes tripped off his tongue!
Lambs to the slaughter. Ah! The little dears.
He fancied a future frisking like a faun,
As lithe as twenty in a golden dawn.

Uncle Max's Mandolin

Max's mandolin was cracked, though firmly
Glued. He'd taken tuners from another lute;
Its tinny tone was less than richly Regal,
Though it bore that moniker on its neck.
He'd picked it up he didn't remember where,
Though that was neither here nor there. Chicago
In the twenties, he traveled everywhere,
Racking up the miles in his Lincoln Touring
Car. He kept posters of his poses in his wrestling togs,
Black socks and shiny shoes went with the job.
So did letting other mobsters know
Those rippling muscles weren't just for show,
His hands so huge and thick I would have bet
There wasn't any way he could finger a fret.

Requiem for a Boxer

"I do it for the money."

Kimbo Slice is dead. His fist
Will long be missed.
A child of Nassau,
Who scoffed at laws,
He fought in parking lots,
Office suites, boxing
Rings and weed-choked plots.
He beat down Afro Puff
And almost every tough
He faced. At forty-four,
He took no more.
His heart gave out.
He lost that bout.
What made Kimbo fight?
What mental night,
What racial blight
Closed other doors
To wealth and worth?
What fired his Homeric—
His Wagnerian mirth?
Now his eternal face,
Bruised though grinning wide,
Suffused with brutal pride—
It's every place,
A fixture of the web,
Though he is dead.

In Memory of Mama's

Second and Bell, Seattle

Mosaics, shattered glass, mirror fragments
Cemented in the street, the door, the walls.
Elvis in plaster, plastic, photos and posters.
Maps of Tenochtitlan and East L.A.
For Dias de los Muertos, Christmas lights!
Coca Cola! Rich and thick with syrup!
Who set the valves? Who modified the mixture?
What genius brewed the salsa, hot and sour?
Crafted the sculpture of the steel fly?
Spake the warning above the bowl of mints?
"Use the spoon or we will use the knife!"
Such loyal waiters down the years!
Their bright tattoos augmented and enhanced in hue.
Pendejo! No marble frieze or Grecian urn
Shall outlast in sabor her crisp taquitos!
Silencio! All honor to Mama's Mexican Kitchen!

Muscat

Sultanate of Oman

Shocking crimson birds with emerald wings
Flit from palm to palm along the shore.
Pale green waves wash the ochre sand;
A haze obscures two islets masked by mist;
Bare red mountains reflect the rising heat.
Under shade, behind a chalky pillar,
A silent vendor sets out chipped white cups.
Cracked cardamom and coffee boil,
Frothing from his tarnished copper pot.
Stoking a stone oven, a bare-armed baker
Eyes a stack of bread rounds thin as wafers
Near a plate of dates dusted with cumin.
Raising one blackened hand in supplication,
The frankincense factor rakes his pile
Of dark gold crystals. The souk awakes.

Hanoi

The exquisitely uniformed policeman in bright white
Gloves performs his dance of waves and gestures.
Yellow lights count down each passing second.
Drivers jam the crossing in all directions.

Bundles of black wires hang above the street
Suspended from steel towers at every corner.
Each shop employs its own extension cord.

The crevices in Buddha's statue hold folded notes,
Crisp Dong displaying the face of Ho Chi Minh,
Or stubs of joss sticks, sharp and black.

An odor of coal permeates the market.
The scarves and jackets smell like sticky tar.

Our translator describes his year in prison
After Saigon fell, his feet in stocks,
His brother's death, his chance escape,
The live grenade he brandished to induce
The captain not to dump his listing boatload
Of refugees in the China Sea. Now
His American passport permits him to return,
Though every hour he seethes.

One Grandfather

It takes a will to comprehend the past,
Even barely. A span now of five
Generations. How to convey an image
Of what I've never seen, that village,
Dylongowska, a bend in a dirt road,
Some scrubby fields circled by thick forests.
How a battered boy of fourteen ran away
And joined the Austro-Hungarian cavalry, trained
To be a butcher and a chef, cooked the stews
At Pod Baranami, 'Under the Head
Of the Ram,' the Socialist café,
In the medieval heart of Krakow, lived
With his young family in old monastery
Cells, skulls and bones firmly plastered
Into the walls of the dusky corridors,
Until he fled to Hamburg and across the Atlantic
To Chicago's stockyards. He built a beanery
To feed the stock men, made head cheese
And Krakowska. His cousins died in Auschwitz
Or in the woods. A few last letters
From Danzig told the news. His café failed.
A final glimpse: a grey man stumbling
Back to a brick apartment block. Snow,
An alcoholic daze. He spoke no English.

Parrots

South Pasadena

At first a pair, escaped and free,
Bright green in the tall bamboo
Next door, where the sly widow
Lived with her disabled son,
The yard not kept since the Japanese
Gardener took his life, unwilling
To go to the camps. The parrots pecked
At fruit from trees gone wild:
Oranges, avocados black and ripe,
Quinces, lemons, fat rose hips,
Grapefruit, figs and tiny limes.
Now, half a century on,
Emerald flocks burst across
The sky like lightning strikes.
The redwood mansion and its urban jungle
Have passed, like the Nisei housemaid
Who lodged in the wide garage.
The parrots have naturalized themselves.
Their viridian wings fly free.

On Lamplight

After the war, for long, dim years
We lived in half-light, like gas light:
One bulb per room, enough to see
And read a book held low beneath
A lamp. Twisting on and off
A knurled switch was a precious treat
For a child, the glow a work of magic,
The filament a flaming wonder,
And a bulb burnt out momentous.
A distant city bureau traded
Good for bad bulbs in fierce Chicago,
Where every action bore political
Weight. You stored dead bulbs before
You dared approach authority:
Lamps stayed dark for tedious months.
One did not wish to face a stern
Official who might ask about your life
Or hint you wasted like a profligate.
Bulbs by rule were traded watt
For watt. No increase was allowed.
How striking our mother's joy
When she learned that in the Golden State
Light bulbs sold at the grocery store.
Films cast light on that era of Noir:
The green-shaded desk lamp, the dark
Foyer, the splendor of the ballroom
Lit up brightly so that jewels could shine:
Wild extravagance in penurious
Periods, careful and saving times,
When energy was scarce and dear,
And the oft-repeated mantra: Turn off
All the lights when you leave the room.

Proletarian Poet

Mr. Harry Goldfarb, Cobbler,
Lived alone behind his Landis
Shoe Machine, an iron monster.
Its whirling shaft spun buffing
Wheels waxed black and brown, steel
Brushes, blades, and polishing stones.
In the near dark, behind the grimy,
Opaque windows, a cloud of rubber
Dust arose at each opening
Of the thick glass door. A tinkling
Steel bell announced your entry.
Boxes of rubber and leather heels
And soles filled cluttered shelves. A chair
Invited customers who chose to wait.
Glue and nails, awls and needles
Tasked his grey-haired hands
That plied this timeless trade, soon
To go the way of typewriter repair.
Across Mission Street, by the Meridian
Iron Works, a horse trough built
Of river rock accumulated
Drying leaves. The Santa Fe
Still stopped at the small station
Shaded by arching robusta palms.
A corner of Goldfarb's window displayed
His miniscule book of verse.
His poems neither rhymed nor scanned,
But rambled in impassioned prose.
Just three inches by five, the chapbook
Raised eyebrows in that Republican town.

World peace, United Nations,
Hatred for war, cooperation
And disarmament, the 'soft soap'
Of a Wobblie or a 'fellow traveler.'
Refugee or Holocaust survivor,
He claimed the title of a poet.

Tanka

Asked about the painting, at first she froze.
'I gave my niece a horse, one I chose.
She tumbled off and broke her neck, and then
Her parents never spoke to me again.
Within a year they both succumbed to cancer.'
Before such utter grief, what could I answer?
Bereft and gutted, she traveled to Tibet,
Where once she studied primates beneath aretes.
Her tale rapt a Lama. In tantric trance
For seven days he painted, sustained by chants:
In a cave, below, a child sat in rue.
Above, the sky erupted cerulean blue.
One hundred monks, kneeling in silent bliss
Circled the Buddha on his blooming lotus.
'Your niece stays now in Bardo,' the Lama said,
'You may rest in peace. Her spirit is fed.'
The tanka hung in shadow on the wall.
Her story had come in fitful bursts. Sweet gall.
A stranger's act of sacrificial kindness
Had brought a measure of numbing rich forgiveness.

Flying Fortress

For J.W.

His dream, at 90, was to parachute,
To leave a plane and enter open air,
Float in freedom, landing anywhere,
Without his heated aviator's suit,
The one he wore for 37 missions,
Including that second famous raid on Schweinfurt,
Although his first flight permanently hurt.
If only he had switched waist-gun positions,
His mentor might have lived—but wait—
For then his blood would have carmined all the crew.
He wished that he could think of something new,
Control the urge to talk, to ruminate.
Never better. Why did doctors lie?
All he wanted was to burst the hatch and fly.

Quercus

California Oaks

Carrying capacity.
How much a natural space can bear.
What terrain and climate reveal
About the limits set on life.
Consider these rolling yellow hills
Of California—from coastal cliffs
The chaparral extends beyond
Two shattered ranges, through arid vineyards,
Past desiccated slopes in Firebaugh,
To citrus groves in the low Sierra
Watered by snaking aqueducts.
All zones of hardy native oaks.
Eight species of their kind:
Black and Valley, Scrub and Blue,
Mesa and Coastal, Oregon,
And grandest of them all, the Live Oak,
Whose limbs can stretch improbably,
Turning and twisting, gaining height,
Threatening to fail but holding
Firm in drought and lashing weather.
Often they grow alone atop
Flat mounts or cling to precipitous hillsides
Where runoff seldom lingers,
Cast single dots of shade on sunburnt
Plains, or group as dwarfs in valleys.
Their sparseness, sometimes one in fifty
Acres, declaims that sustenance
Is rare, and the land unfit
For lengthy settlement. These oaks
Thrive best as solitary trees.
Their land is meant for barrenness.

The Home of Truth

At the Home of Truth in Pasadena,
A bare-bones office suite,
I waited for the avatar.
She arrived at last in a Buick sedan,
Pale blue, like her floral dress.
Eager to address her three followers,
She moved behind her lectern like a queen.

The I Am Temple in North Seattle
Seldom unlocks its steel gates.
A picture of the Russian immortal,
Saint Germain, stares at the street
From behind a pane of fly-specked
Glass. Prostitutes linger
Under the generous cover
Of the elaborate plaster portico.

Cao Dai counts among its holy ones
Victor Hugo, who fought for freedom,
Sun Yat Sen, Vladimir Lenin,
Joan of Arc, and a Vietnamese martyr.
Its golden temples grace neighborhoods
Where immigrants have lately settled.

And at a lonely aqua house trailer,
Parked off a road under dusky oaks
In deserted Dulzura, deep in the San
Diego mountains, one might have bought
A copy of the Atheist's Bible. Angry
Believers painted scriptures against
The Anti-Christ on nearby boulders
Along the twisting highway.

Perspectives on the ultimate
Sustain and last when they are most
The same, the way that one and one
Make two, not six. Even grand traditions
Wane and fail when what they teach
Wanders from common truths
Shared among the oldest faiths.
How is it that the deviant maths
Attract believers to their curious paths?

Ideas and Abstractions

Aeschylus Knew Better

Endosymbiosis is the swall-
owing of cell by cell, a cannibal
Routine that, well, allowed the bare prokar-
yote to swell and grow a nucleus,
Which led at last to such as—us,
The multi-celled eukaryotes, who care
Not to associate with sulfurous slime,
Having, we think, served sufficient time
Amongst the lower orders. Aeschylus
Knew better: the House of Atreus
Reveals our autotrophic nature. God
Ate God; Titan, Titan; man his child:
Sheer plod down generations, each fod-
der for the maw of what's still fully wild.

Poetry Weather

Fat vowels like mustachioed porpoises
Squeezed into polka dot bathing suits,
Angular consonants in tasseled brogues
Thrusting walking sticks with steel points.
Peremptory, imperative feet:
The stamping spondee, that angry toddler.
The dactyl dragging its lugubrious tail
Where a cool September sun breaks
The crest of a rude and rocky ridge.
A tumulus below, stones in a circle
Like supernumerary prepositions
Filling out the dips in a deadly bog.
Slithering weather, good for a quick glissade
Down snow or scree at senseless speed.
Blazing light, lungfulls of pulsing air.

Henge

I built a henge in my front yard.
Six Pennsylvania bluestones and a granite knob
Set on compass points, at the East a limestone shard.
Dug in ivy for eternity,
Mint for sweet times and thyme for hard.
We hung St. George's cross from a laurel tree,
Drank mead and whisky to salute the bard,
And spoke old Caedmon's hymn to bless the job,
No Trinity or Jesus, just praise for Heaven's guard,
With a nod to Frea, the maternal twin of God.
Crows and finches wheel,
Tendrils twist and dart,
Circle calls to circle,
Maker gladdens heart.

Poetry Time

Our time expands or shrinks as we create
Or waste our hours in passive idleness.
To pause and wait is not to hesitate:
How fruitful a day of disciplined emptiness.
The sun rises and sets, the lavender blooms,
Bees scour the petals of open flowers
Sampling pollen for their honeycombs.
The breeze brings clouds and welcome showers.
Digressions and guesses play out their games of chess,
Ideas and calculations surge and ebb,
Ineffable mix of blanks and consciousness.
Thoughts and sounds and colors spin a web.
A poem assembles, cinema crystalized
That screens in myriad ways behind our eyes.

Communion

Time was, people had control: autonomy
Over autos. On regular Sundays, like priests,
We prostrated ourselves before our beloved idols,
Raised a chassis on creaking jacks, blocked
The grounded tires with chunks of wood or bricks,
Inserted rusty jack-stands, and began the rite.
The altar was ready. First the drain plug,
Then the valves, adjusted tight with slippery
Feeler gauges, spark plugs brushed and gapped,
Points freshly filed. Saints provided
Essential parts. Manny, Moe and Jack,
The trinity of Pep Boys, offered unction
By the quart. A timing light confirmed
The consummation of the ritual—
Unless confession revealed a need for special
Absolutions: Marvel Mystery Oil,
STP, Motor Honey, or a junk yard
Run for salvaged parts. Well-tuned, the machine
Made us feel prepared, deeply clean,
And blessed with skills to face a broken world.

Objecting

"We were all conscientious objectors,"
The veteran said, hiding from the fireworks
That Fourth of July. Explosions brought on flashbacks
Of the night he was "blown away" by a mortar shell
On his first patrol in rural Vietnam.
I could have explained my deep religious convictions,
Though I knew he understood far better
A different insight. Not about our nation's
Dark economy, or Congress' failure
To vote on any war, but something simpler,
The battering of souls, the training to repress
Our basic instincts to care and help and love.
We sat inside and scanned the TV channels.
They reinforced the training once again.

QED (Quantum Electrodynamics)

Feynman found that photons flow
In all directions, quaquaversely.
Some fly up beneath your toes,
Others shoot behind, reversely.
Light is no directional ray,
But fields of vectors, wild at play.

Near Telegraph

On the banks of Strawberry Creek,
Beside the grove of redwoods, tall
And redolent in the summer heat,
August of '68, the rill is
Low and slow yet flowing still.
A haze of gas, sparkling shards
Of shattered window glass shine
From Telegraph, a taste
Of pepper on the tongue, a waste,
This trashing of a neighborhood
Intent on change and good.
Dogs plash and play. My love,
Can we create the land we seek?

On the Anniversary of People's Park

Berkeley, 1969

Streets are for speed, land for construction:
These are the inalienable rights,
And all your talk of Jefferson,
Cyclical revolution, popular ownership,
And calls to paternal authorities

Were resolved by the President, who in '63
Admonished us that recourse to speech,
Parades and protest was a tragedy,
An excess understandable among the blacks,
But not to be condoned, the first amendment
A safety valve, not a rule, and

The thirty percent of land immured
In tar that taints our water—those possible playfields,
Farm plots, dramatic spaces, historic digs—
Ceded to commerce, and the public squares to silence,
Inestimable evidence of our achieved communal bliss.

As curfew closes all the urban spaces,
Cruisers by squads of three patrol the streets,
Sheriffs in masks retrieve spent gas grenades,
A burning haze drifts toward the Bay.
Only the state can build a park.

Oud

An oud is a pear,
Long-stemmed,
With a neck grotesquely bent,
And a belly
Striped like a circus tent.
Its eleven strings,
Ten in pairs,
Invite marauding fingers
To play Middle Eastern airs,
Though whatever tunes it sings
Echo with a buzz that lingers.
A trill on the oud may portend
Riffs that shake bellies to jelly.
Beware.
If Eric Satie or Alfred Jarry
Had been aware,
We might have had Oud Roi
Or three ouds in the shape of une poire.
Et Marcel Duchamp? Parfait!
An oud descending an escalier.

Baglama

The Turkish baglama, also called a saz.
Produces music like cool solo jazz.
Fretted in arresting quarter tones,
The lower strings beget hypnotic drones.
Songs unfold as complex variations
Of Arabic 'makams' assembled into keys
That challenge, puzzle, confound, and sometimes please.
Jazz grew from the sufferings of a race.
Sufis play the saz to free a space
For meditations, dance and centering prayers.
Interlocking melodies remove the layers
Of mundane fears and troubles. Stripped bare,
Minds lie open to sober revelations
Of fundamental truths both wise and rare.

Swallow

Swine wallow,
Frogs bellow,
Fish swallow,
Swallows glide,
Chipmunks chide.
Deep or shallow,
Every hollow
To something hallowed.
Fallow fields hide
Callow creatures;
Raptors seek
Their telltale features.
Swoop and swallow,
Squirm and squeak.
No longer yellow,
That bloodied beak.

Euler's Identity

The question is what to make of i,
A number that perplexes. Why?
It can't exist, a contradiction
That points, in fact, to a new dimension.
Zero, its transcendental peer,
Has a feature just as queer.
Zero is both none and one:
One minus minus one is two, not none.
Cartesian coordinates lay it out,
And zero factorial removes all doubt.
Euler foreshadowed Gödel's proof:
Every system puts the lie to its truth.
When joined to pi and natural e,
Whose digits run random to eternity,
The imaginary number's logic fits
Plane geometric sines. His wits
Amazed, Feynman swore he saw
In Euler how God made law.

I am Life and Death

Professor Urey, a pacifist,
Deserves a special Guinness list.
He won the Nobel Prize for finding water—
Not H_2O, the normal stuff—
But H_3O: if you have enough
You can separate two kinds of matter,
The isotopes of uranium,
And presto! You can make the Bomb.
Next, he unveiled the emergence of life.
He and Stan Miller filled a flask
With water, a spark, and common gasses.
The amino acids soon got rife,
Which showed the universe is built
To birth both paradox and guilt.

Dame Julian

"And all manner of things shall be well."

It strains credulity to believe in good.
The maid, a refugee, trembled as she stood,
'All gone,' she stuttered, 'sisters, brothers,
Mother. I came from Lanka. All the others . . . '
She spoke in French with awkward intonation.
Forgiveness would bring no reconciliation.
At the Place des Vosges, a march for Palestine.
Gendarmes maintained a fluid containment line.

Sri Joshi, over dinner, recounted his posts,
United Nations missions to bloody revolts:
Baghdad, Kabul, Zimbabwe, Cote D'Ivoire,
Attacks, invasions, reigns of public horror.
He set aside two hours each day
To study Bhagavad-Gita and to pray.
A Bhakti, he put his faith in human care.
'May the Lord be with you,' he said, laying bare
The absence of distance between us, mere masks
Of the same embodiment, identical tasks.

One summer day, as cloud wisps slowly sailed,
Engulfed. Swallowed by the numinous whale.
A limitless invitation, boundless calm,
Julian's words remembered, lasting balm.

Variation on Verses from Jonah and Job

The numinous whale, no mythical beast,
Swallows us whole, felicitous feast.
Fearsome in frolics, though not keen to destroy,
It claims it transfigures sorrow to joy.
The waves of its wake leave open, behind,
Bright and becalmed a path for the mind.

That Tree

No one can take this away:
That night, alone and four
Years old, clad warmly in a girl's
Pink coat, tramping through snow
Around the block at midnight.
Safe outdoors. Puzzled by the way
Those buttons worked, not as on other clothes.
Afraid to go inside, peering
At the lights in houses where icicles
Reflected gaudy Christmas colors.
Leafless branches, the scent of coal,
Cars weighted with chrome parked
Deep in their drives, a nose-burning
Wind, a trash can clattering in the dark.
That tree. The only conifer.
Still it grows, a century now.
Flocked with fresh flakes, conical
In form, straight, precise and perfect.
If order there, then everywhere.

Teaching

Undergrads, those four assistants
Who blossomed—joy and skill and tact.
The first, her seeing eye dog gnawed
The classroom carpet. The 'little person'
Never spoke of pain from swollen joints.
The junior with Duchennes who drove
His power chair with feeble fingers.
And the last, who could move
Only a single thumb and digit
Before her mouth: she joked and bantered.
Soon the freshmen saw
Just free and agile minds.

It is What it Is

He sat across the table and explained
How the tumor had spread throughout his brain.
His intelligence, he said, was fading fast,
And motor control had lately passed.
His hands, when they were out of sight,
Refused to do his will, try as he might.
With patients he'd been very terse.
Now, just as bluntly, he faced the worst.
His gaze direct, he said goodbye.
He just had time to close his lab and die.

Bad Times

It is a broken land, full of fissures
And faults. Slavery, rape, and genocide,
Exclusions and expulsions, fratricide,
Walls and fences, poverty inducing measures.
Quakes are common, and when they shake the earth,
Aftershocks unsettle dangerous rabble.
Loners shoot down crowds of men like battle.
And now the weather. Famine follows dearth
With fishless seas. Suddenly a flood:
Cascades of tumbling rocks, scarlet mud,
Rivers of rubble crashing through doors,
Surging waves of whelming civic horrors,
Verbal violence, red-faced angry jeers,
Daily lies that pander to primal fears.

Glass Butte, Oregon

What drives diggers to search in shallow shafts?
Beneath the shade of a western juniper
We sipped at stubby glasses of smoked Mezcal.
The air was dry, the elevation high.
Tired of working in other rock-hounds' digs,
We scavenged among the glinting chips that lay
Around a fire pit, knapping knives
From shining shards, our hammers bits of rock
And wood. Flakes of obsidian splintered and flew.
Prying in the Earth's alembic affirms
The glory of this planet's chemistry:
Atop this peak, so many volcanic glasses,
Mahogany and lace, black and rainbow,
Gold sheen, pumpkin, red, and double flow—
And all the plants that drive their hardy roots
Down through this soil that dusts our weathered boots.

The Artichoke

The glaucous green leaves of the artichoke
Spin its spearpoint symmetry, a finial
Fit for a courtly garden gate.
Once deconstructed to litter on a plate,
Stripped of all their tartly flavored pulp,
The segments curl and turn translucent,
Embedded in waves of cold, congealed oil.
Cut away the choke's sharp spears:
The stalk reveals the heart, the fount
Of lingering, piquant, subtle savor.
This bud, this stingless thistle, this fangless favor.

General Education

You would not ask a poet to compose a rhyme
In haste: why ask a freshman to compose
A Weltanschauung as if it were a pose?
This courtship requires years of idle time.
Enough to test the sinews of some books,
Defend a proposition in debate,
Learn to eye a concept by its date,
Be tempted by conversion's piercing hooks.
Experiences in depth, substantial papers
Twice revised, a guided dalliance
With bitter error—this is the knife-edged dance
Of mind and nubile faith, the fateful caper.
How shall they know the truly meretricious,
Unless they taste ideas both rich and vicious?

September 1, 2019

It's been eighty years
To this time of the terrible buffoons.
At least the last lot
Learned their lines. Hitler
Would never have said covfefe,
Or come on stage with his hair
Uncombed, like babbling Boris.
Atom bombs and holocausts
Are hideous, but the rising sea
Will wash whole states away,
Nor all the frozen lakes
Of Canada supply
The widening Sahel.
The weather will not surrender
Aboard the old Missouri.
Is it too late to save ourselves?
Wystan, your affirming flame
Has left a carbon footprint.

Canzone

Supposing Jesus to be wise, to forgive
Prompts moral transformation, hence his advice
Fits well within the objectives of the law
And no way undermines a flourishing state.
Nor are mercy and absolution foolish.
Victims and offenders often reconcile,
And peace so firmly grounded ends all fights.

How controversial this mandate to forgive,
Enlightenment philosophers sternly advise.
Absolution grossly flouts all sense of law,
Erodes true justice sanctioned by the state,
And renders those who forgive completely foolish.
Actions and laws must perfectly reconcile.
Surrendering never stops a fight.

Besides, it is false that those who heal, first forgive.
Allowing time for anger is wise advice.
Often it is better to trust to the law,
And invoke the sober power of the state.
Letting felons free to rampage is foolish.
It is truth and safety we must reconcile
To bring an end to private and public fights.

Yet forgiving blesses most those who forgive.
For personal health one should therefore advise
Acts that heal the self—even against the law.
After all, what is the basis of the state
If not the good of people? Is it foolish
To start with personal peace and reconcile
The law to our own well-being to end all fights?

Bishop Butler opined that reasons to forgive
Were hotly debated. Was such an act advised
Now that Locke had laid a fresh basis for the law
And worked to reformulate the civil state?
In radical times, was it not just foolish
Statecraft and Christian faith to reconcile
After so many decades of religious fights?

Dr. King and Tolstoy said we must forgive.
Gandhi advised that faiths should reconcile.
Could the law and the state be truly foolish?

Holy

The white spotted puffer fish
That swims in shallow Asian seas
Creates a sunburst sculpture in the sand
To attract a mate. Symmetrical,
Complex, hundreds of times its puny size—
And whisks it all away
In an instant, as if a trifle.
Perhaps its creation captures how the puffer
Sees the sun through blue-green waves.
Bower birds build bold
Monuments adorned with colored
Stones, scavenged glass and stolen
Beads—For Darwin part of a mystery
Far deeper than simple survival: the codes
And rites of sexual selection.
Crows use tools and long remember
Those who pique their enmity.
Dolphins speak in clicks, whales
Sing and moan, and their distant cousins
The hostile hippopotami
Clack loudly to each other in the muddy
Depths of African rivers. Elephants
Grieve, die for their young, and mark out
Mausoleums. Pass beyond
These testaments to feral wisdom
To their luminous sense of place:
Gorillas in Gabon gather to greet
Hollow stumps that they strike with far
Flung rocks, like pilgrims on the Hajj
Stoning the devil, while pachyderms
Congress at the rising of the moon,
Waving broken branches at the celestial body,

Like priests asperging or Houngans sprinkling
Their congregants with blood from headless
Chickens. Fish school in spherical
Patterns beyond the imagining
Of entranced and dancing dervishes.
What part of common evolution
Is awareness of the holy?

Design

I saw a tiny spider descend,
And wondered what it might portend.
I'd never seen that species there.
Its presence laid my study bare.
A change in fauna, so close, at home.
The climate alters, the animals roam.
A silken, silver thread so fine.
A leaden, numbing warning sign.

Baby Boomer

Disneyland

Frontierland attracted me first,
With its sinuous caves.
Adventureland's Asian rivers came next:
The play of guns and travel.
Lately I sit at the French Market
Idling over espresso
While my children board the riverboat.
One day I will hobble along Main Street,
Stand at the arcade,
And see the castle from afar.
Some other fantasy follows,
Virgil, written by another artist.

Covid 19, or The Revenge of the Pangolin

The pangolin,
A scaly beast,
Curls into a ball.

Armored without,
Tender within,
Not edible at all.

Unless you catch
One unawares
And penetrate its wall.

So sad it bears
A virus that
Casts a global pall.

Envoy: Now Rose

At your funeral, the pastor praised
The way you gathered the parish women
To proselytize for married sex. No man
Complained he lacked for love, the minister said,
A first among his churches. The congregation
Whispered you were the horniest old couple!
You took an equal joy in every task,
Always giggling under your breath
As if the world were one great joke.
You couldn't pronounce Mukilteo, the ferry
Stop, without breaking into laughter,
And you always found something to praise in the early drafts
Of those Christian writers you drew to you each year.
You held right Baptist core beliefs, though
Your heart had room for every human creed.
There was darkness, too. Your step dad
Blew his head off when diabetes
Left him impotent. The shotgun
Blast tattooed the walls with brains and gore.
And when you cast away your farmer's speech,
Aiming to earn a PhD—with five unruly
Kids—you sewed a litter of kittens into a pillow
Case and threw them in a stormy lake.
Still, mirth and hope prevailed. You knew
There is something more. Barefoot mountain Rose,
Soft dust cushioning your curling toes,
You turned your college classrooms into shady groves
Where flights of words and images flitted about,
Finding their proper perches in rhythmic lines
That you annotated—poems and papers—in script
Enhanced by rows of exclamation marks.

Old Poems

To the Last Professor, Denying Tenure, For Jean Facing Cancer, Dear Dr. Faustus, Sonnet, Lambley Priory: *Christianity and Literature.*

Tyson at the Louvre, Zen Garage Sale, For David Dead of AIDS, Betrayal, Muslin, Near Torrey Pines, Japanese Gardener: *Duckabush Review.*

On Some Recent Critics, On the Street: *Rolling Coulter.*

For Great Uncle Boleslaw, Fifth Column: *Literature of the Oppressed.*

In Transit: *Wallace Stevens Journal.*

For William Oxley of Scarborough: *Bellowing Ark.*

Nor Am I Out of It: *Pontifex.*

At the Ice Cream Parlor: *Perception.*

The Biologist Considers his Career: *Spectrum.*

Schizophrenia: *Light and Life.*

Family Resemblances: *Trestle Creek Review.*

Cannibalism: *Celebration of Poetry.*

Atom Bomb Drill: *Washington English Journal.*

Some of these anthologized in *Second Essence, Christianity and Literature 50 Years of Poetry Special Edition,* and *Imago Dei* (ACU Press, 2012).

www.ingramcontent.com/pod-product-compliance
Lightning Source LLC
Chambersburg PA
CBHW061504040426
42450CB00008B/1482